milk and brexit

quotes overheard and shared by the public

transcribed by

nathan bragg

theresa vogrin

about this book

brexit has divided our country into two factions but there is one thing that connects us all – our humour. therefore, our only intention with this book is to make people laugh and brighten up their day.

milk and brexit is a successive collection of the most iconic quotes and jokes about brexit, overheard in public or on tv, as well as shared across social media platforms like twitter, facebook and instagram.

we hope to have captured the essence of both the leave and remain camps during each stage of the brexit lifecycle that is as politically neutral as it is hilarious.

Cover Design and Art Direction by Nathan Bragg

Illustrations by Theresa Vogrin

Idiocratea is an imprint of Polygon Publishing LTD.

www.polygonpublishing.com

www.idiocratea.com

ISBN-13: 978-1-9163740-0-3

brexit (n)

the undefined being negotiated by the unprepared in order to get the unspecified for the uninformed.

contents

the five stages of brexit grief

DENIAL ANGER BARGAINING DEPRESSION ACCEPTANCE

denial

DENIAL ANGER BARGAINING DEPRESSION ACCEPTANCE

knowing britain
simon cowell
will probably have
the final fucking vote
and take it to deadlock.

brexit?
i love brexit.
it’s great.

it’s the most important meal
of the day.

the only single market
i want to leave
is tinder.

this is a scary
uncertain
divided
result
but i reckon
it would make
an absolutely cracking
episode of
the thick of it.

uh oh
the uk
just changed
its facebook status
to *it's complicated.*

lots of remainers
are deliberately confusing
europe and *eu*.

britain is
officially
leaving europe.
where are they going
to go? how hard
is it to move an
island? well first
they need to have
someone go down and
pull the release level in the
chunnel. that detaches
them from
the mainland
and allows them to
float free. then the
dutch wind farms will turn
their windmills on and blow
the country out into the
ocean where it can catch trade
currents wherever it would like to go.

never trust
anything written
on the side of a bus.

british weather
has never favoured europe.

remember the armada?
1588?

storms in london
may have kept
remain voters
at home.

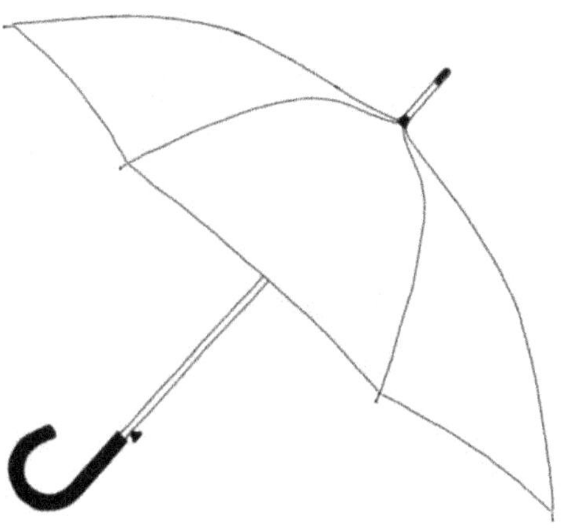

is there an eu referendum
morning-after-pill
that regrexit could access?

let’s go to the winchester
have a pint
and wait for this all
to blow over.

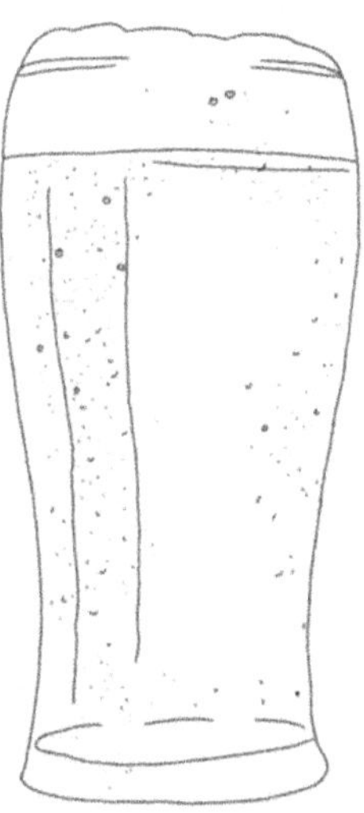

off to the pub
to discuss the eu referendum
and britain's future
with the lads
even though none of us know
what the fuck we're talking about.

after brexit
the police will stop
using german shepherds
and will replace them
with yorkshire terriers.

i seriously believe
theresa may
is having the longest stroke
in the history
of humankind.

the remain camp
would have accepted
the eu referendum result
if they had won.

but they didn't.

so they don't.

petulant children.

brexit is
like a sitcom
where at the start of the episode
the main character
tells a casual lie
about being able to skydive
to impress someone
and now they are
at the end of the episode
in a plane
about to jump.

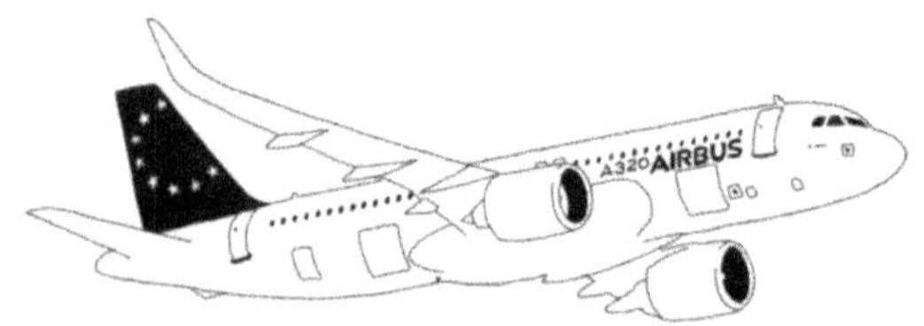

breaking news:

all eu countries
except uk
left the eu
and created
the ea
because it was
easier than brexit.

the question is
leaf or romaine.

i still don’t know
what the benefits of brexit are
and at this point
i’m afraid to ask.

does brexit mean
we don’t have to take part
in that eurovision song contest bollocks
any more?

is there anywhere
in the world
that isn’t laughing
at the british
right now?

have we tried
unplugging 2016
waiting ten seconds
and plugging it back in?

why does the brexiter
have so many children?

because he refuses
to acknowledge
that pulling out never works.

anger

DENIAL ANGER BARGAINING DEPRESSION ACCEPTANCE

brexit
is worse
than comic sans.

so many remoaners
foaming at the mouth
to say something mean
about brexiteers.

sad little muppets.

never forget
that the uk is leaving
the world's biggest trading bloc
and peace project
because hugh and daphne
don't like hearing foreign accents
in their local waitrose.

was in waitrose earlier
when my 8-year-old son
saw someone paying
for the mail on sunday
at the checkout.

he shouted
i hope you realise
you're funding hate,
you stole my future and
i hope you die soon.

i cuffed the little twat
around the ear
and everybody cheered.

hang on
we lost the rugby?

clearly the fault
of us remainers
for not believing hard enough.

only the british
could tyrannically colonise
half the world
then leave the eu
because of immigrants.

who will pick
my blueberries now
if it isn't
some poorly paid foreigner?

those coal mines
will be filled with chagrin
when they next go to waitrose
for a punnet.

hopefully these morons
will crawl back
to their council flats and houses
and not be heard from.

unfortunately for them
they'll have to shop at
tesco, sainsbury's and waitrose,
as they're too british for
aldi and lidl.

i'm not sure
i know any waitrose shoppers
who voted leave.

now aldi and lidl
that's a different matter
rather ironically.

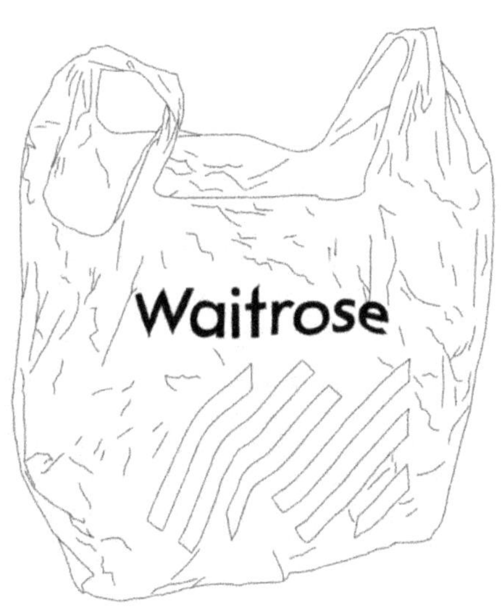

those stupid little people
who voted to leave
should be shot.

will they celebrate
with spanish lager at 11pm?
a bottle of french wine?
get home with an albanian taxi driver?
stop for an italian pizza?
a few more polish beers when back at home
and then picked up by a butch paramedic
to have their stomach pumped
by an austrian doctor in a&e?

brexit is
the dodgy surgeon
who promises you
a penis that'll touch the ground
and delivers it by
chopping off your legs.

it’s been four years
of this shit
and my phone
still feels the need
to correct
brexit to *becky*
every bloody time.

come on man.
i don’t even know
any beckys.

i’d rather cut my own leg off
and beat myself to death
with it
than hear another word
about brexit.

not only
has the uk left the eu
but remainers are now
the loonies and fruitcakes.

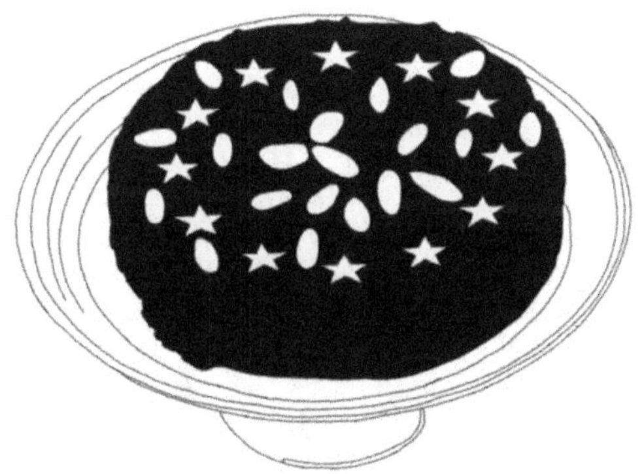

bargaining

DENIAL ANGER BARGAINING DEPRESSION ACCEPTANCE

uk: i'll tell you what i want, what i really, really want.

eu: so tell me what you want, what you really, really want.

uk: i'll tell you what i want, what i really, really want.

eu: so tell me what you want, what you really, really want.

(repeat for 28 months)

when you are at a party
and you spend four hours
unsure how to leave
that is called a brexit.

in and out
is a very hard decision.

it's like the other day
my flatmate was making me
a peppermint tea
and he said
would you like the bag
left in
or taken out?

if you leave the bag in
as a whole the cup of tea itself
will get stronger
and it might appear
that the bag is getting weaker
but it is now part
of a stronger cup of tea.

whereas if you take the bag out
the tea is now quite weak
but the bag itself
goes directly in the bin.

- james acaster

the year is 2192.

the british prime minister
visits brussels
to ask for an extension
of the brexit deadline.

no one remembers
where this tradition originated
but every year
it attracts many tourists
from all over the world.

i deal with
tough mathematical questions
every day,
but please don't ask me
to help with brexit!

- *stephen hawking*

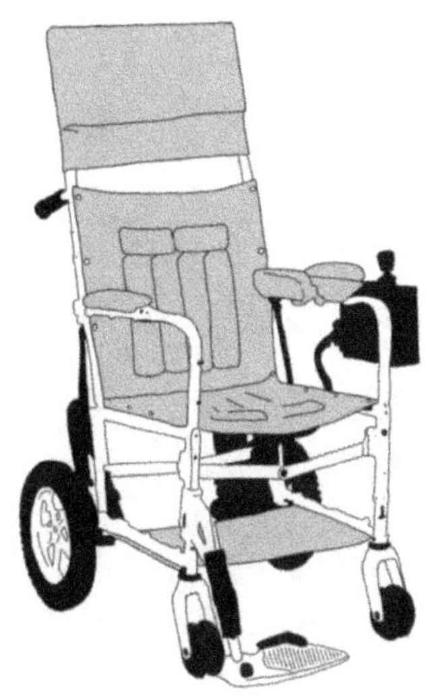

theresa may
writes brexit letter to eu:

i have no idea
what i'm doing.
lol

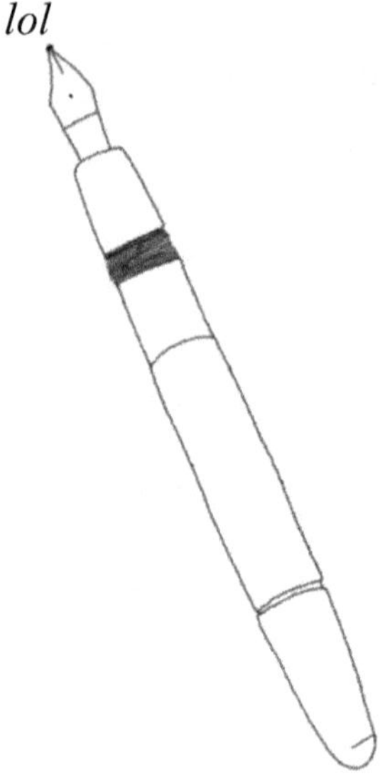

knock knock.

who's there?

brexit.

brexit who?

it is not my job
to tell you that.
work it out for yourself.

will i even
get let back
into the uk
with this tan
if we've left
the eu
by the time
i am back?

me: hey cat,
what's your opinion
on the uk and brexit?

cat: i think
they should repeatedly ask
to leave
but then when the door is open
just sit there and stare at it.
that's what i would do.

two years later:

britain: *listen, we made a mistake.*

eu: *new phone, who dis?*

i'm considering
cutting back my pizza eating
due to the uncertainty of brexit.

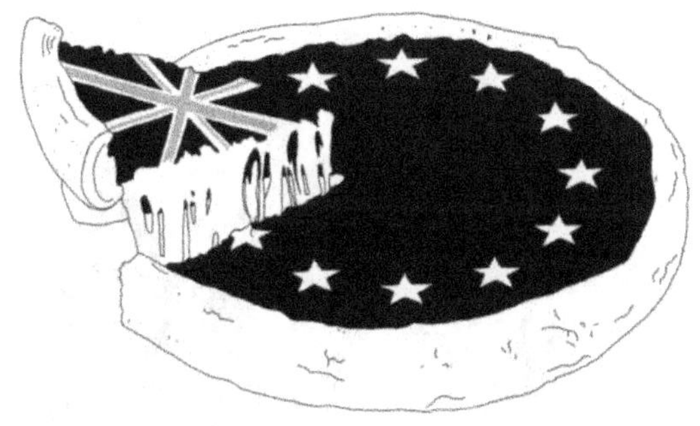

there is going to be
a 50p coin
commemorating brexit.
it's nearly done.

they just can't decide
what to do with the border.

brexit will make
prices go up
in britain.
so it will cost them
twice as much
to not go to the dentist.

- conan o'brien

eu: let the brexiters go to hell.

uk: hell is empty.

eu: that's right, all the demons are right here.

uk: that's one more reason for us to leave the eu.

soft brexit / hard brexit

basically just
a married couple
arguing over
if they're off out
or off out out.

brexit is
the worst trade negotiation since
star wars: the phantom menace.

alexa, how is brexit
doing today
after all the negotiations?

jesus christ.
the same.
yesterday,
today
and forever.

a brexit deal
could take ten years.

that's not fair.

most of the people
who voted for it
could be dead by then.

- *gary lineker*

can we have
a referendum
for london
to leave the uk?

if a second referendum is
letting the people decide
then what was
the first referendum?

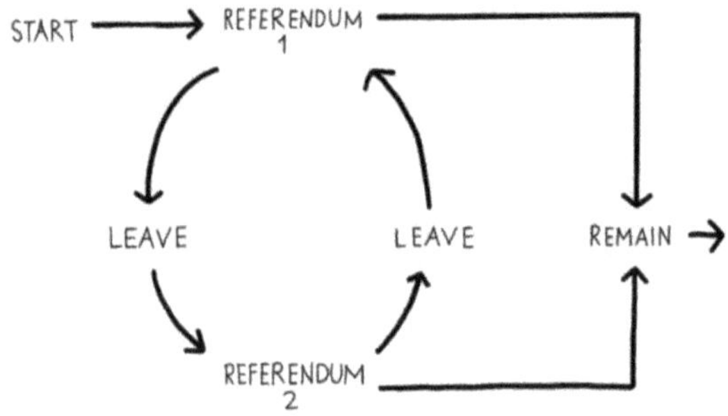

we had brexit, yes.

but what about second brexit?

depression

DENIAL ANGER BARGAINING DEPRESSION ACCEPTANCE

i long for the simpler days
when brexit
was just a term
for leaving brunch early.

no longer part of the eu.
no prime minister.
pound fucked.

what a fucking shit friday this is.

tonight
brexiteers will
creep down stairs
and steal the dreams
hopes and wishes
of future generations.

darling
we'll have to start
stockpiling french cheese
now that brexit is happening.

- *mother to her daughter*

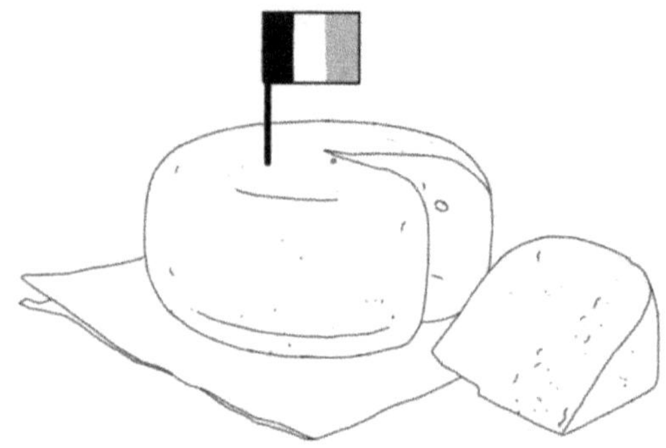

but darling
absolutely everyone in davos
was positively quivering
with fear
about the shortage of gluten-free dhmo
after brexit.

what’s the opposite of
freedom of movement?

arthritis.

some famous deaths in 2016:

alan rickman
david bowie
victoria wood
prince
the uk

britain's brexit plan
reminds me of
the time the school's roof collapsed
and we sold
rice crispy cakes
because we were ten
and had no other skills.

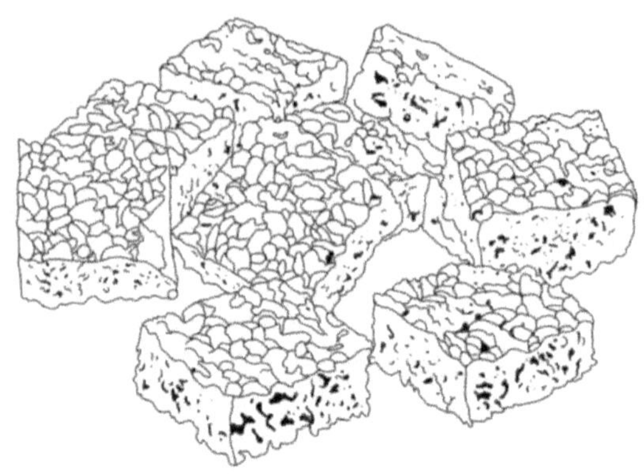

say goodbye
to croissants, people.

delicious croissants.

we are stuck
with crumpets forever.

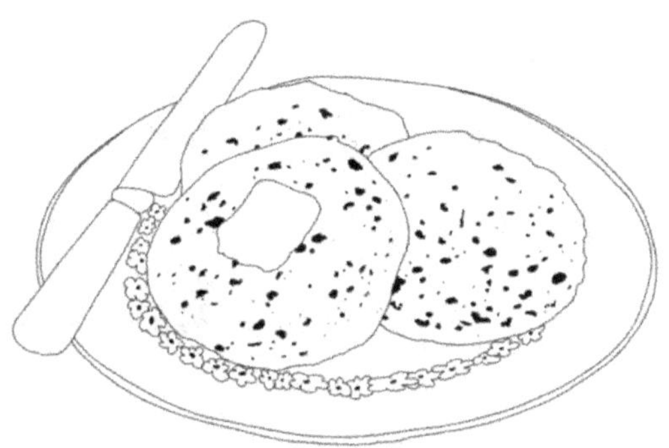

sales of gin
have doubled.

prescriptions for antidepressants
are up 30%.

how will christmas dinner
be different after brexit?

no brussels.

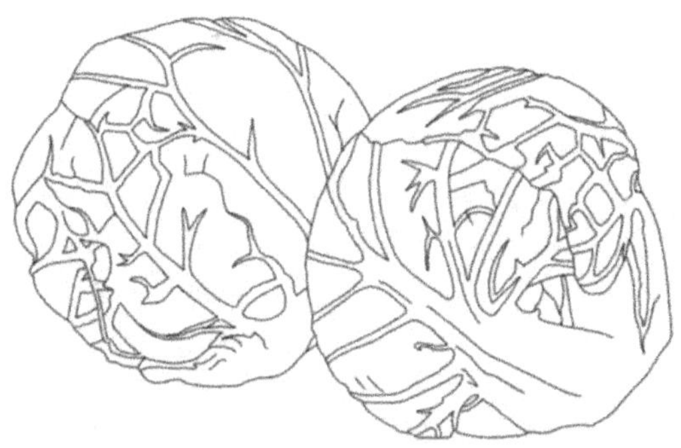

the paper quality
of waitrose christmas cards
doesn’t seem to equal last years.

brexit must have hit hard.

wrestled an old lady
for the last piece of camembert
in waitrose.

it just doesn't taste the same
outside the eu.

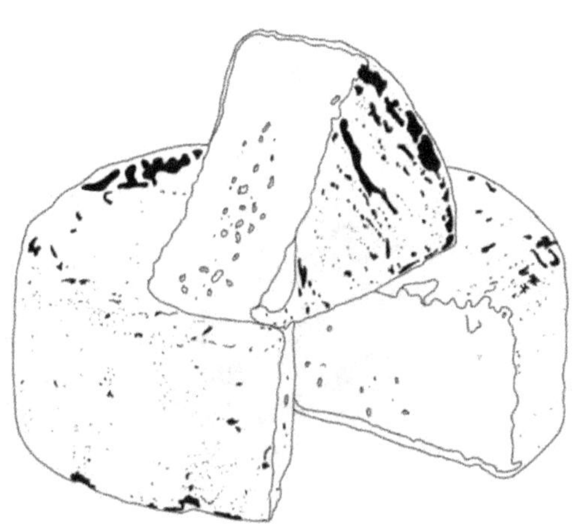

i've left my brexit eve shopping
to the very end.
worried that the shops
will have run out of humbug
and chlorinated chicken.

still at least
the sovereignty has arrived.

don’t forget to prepare
your brexit eve boxes
for the kids.

new pyjamas,
tinned meat,
anti-depressants
and hope.

i'm going to go
on a brexit diet.

the pounds will drop fast.

after brexit
when rapper 50 cent
performs in gbr
he will appear as 10.000 pounds.

merkel announced
that in the event of no deal
sales to the uk
of sausage and cheese
would cease immediately.

but that would be
the wurst käse scenario.

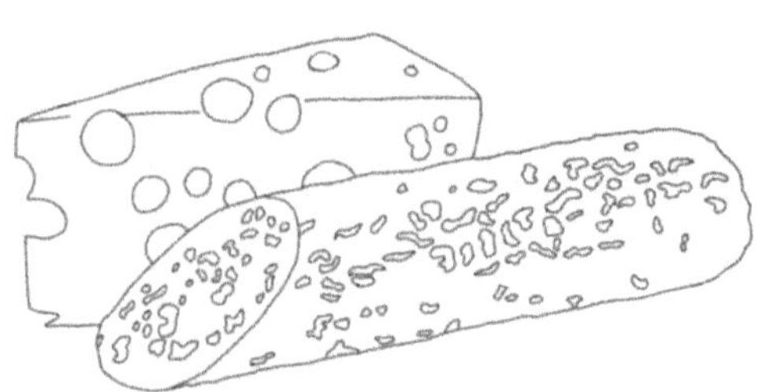

it's brexit eve.

all is lost.
i have no tears left to cry.

from here on
we shall all be forced
to wait slightly longer
before getting on a flight
that we shouldn't even be getting on
because of climate change.

sad day.

acceptance

DENIAL ANGER BARGAINING DEPRESSION ACCEPTANCE

i'm really enjoying
the season finale of *the uk*.

i was angry about
the whole brexit
and free movement thing
but then i realised
i haven't been on a holiday
since 2012
and i'm broke anyway
so how much worse can it get?

- *kae kurd*

england?
*out*gland more like!

with britain
leaving the eu
how much space was created?

exactly 1 gb.

what did britain say
to its trade partners?

see *eu* later.

the next james bond film
will just be him
spending 2 hours
in passport control.

i'm marrying
a canadian chick anyways
and moving there,
so do whatever
you all want.

t'was the day before brexit
and it was now so clear
there had been no need
for that project of fear.

my first post brexit visit to the uk.

entered without visa,
but big changes here.

people drive on the wrong side
of the road
and can’t pay with euros!

post brexit tesco
is full of food,
i can buy petrol,
my daughter has booked a holiday.

stop fucking moaning
and support other countries
that cannot even get
fresh water.

you’re boring me.

brexiteers
are a lot hotter
than remainers.

fact.

bong, bong, bong.
brexit day is here.

goodbye eu –
mind the gap!

why does britain
like tea
so much?

because tea leaves.

britain has no master
britain is a free elf!

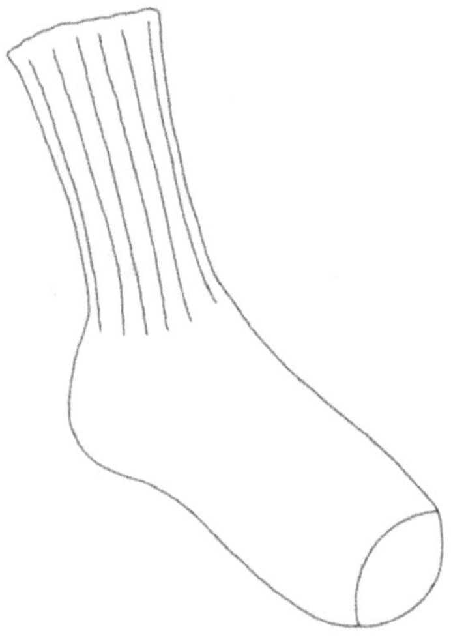

how did you vote? said pooh.
leave, said piglet.
i voted remain, said pooh.

are we still friends? said piglet.
yes… yes we're still friends, said pooh.

good, said piglet.
let's go to the pub and get pissed.

if you enjoyed *milk and brexit*
please consider leaving a review
on amazon

thank you.

other books published by *idiocratea*:

overheard at waitrose
overheard at waitrose II
overheard at whole foods
google search poetry

about this book

brexit has divided our country into two factions but there is one thing that connects us all – our humour. therefore, our only intention with this book is to make people laugh and brighten up their day.

milk and brexit is a successive collection of the most iconic quotes and jokes about brexit, overheard in public or on tv, as well as shared across social media platforms like twitter, facebook and instagram.

we hope to have captured the essence of both the leave and remain camps during each stage of the brexit lifecycle that is as politically neutral as it is hilarious.

idiocratea doesn't hold the copyright to the words, only to the illustrations and the presentation of the quotes. all credits go to the people who uttered and posted the contents of this book. we tried our best to include all of them in the list on the following pages.

credits to

- @acciojess on twitter (page 9)
- @Leitchy03 on twitter (page 12)
- @Leo_Flanagan on twitter (page 13)
- @markcritch on twitter (page 14)
- @MoodySlayerUK on twitter (page 15)
- @888sport on twitter (page 17)
- @msl_johnson on twitter (page 18)
- @Nayabnasir on twitter (page 19)
- @Seapeekay on twitter (page 20)
- @SwearingTravel on twitter (page 21)
- @kerbcrab on twitter (page 22)
- @LiarMPs on twitter (page 23)
- @HandofGOD7 on twitter (page 24)
- @Ullger_art on twitter (page 25)
- @cbettinelli87 on twitter (page 27)
- @James_Buckley on twitter (page 28)
- @dongwon on twitter (page 30)
- @ahhayor on twitter (page 31)
- @roosku on twitter (page 35)
- @antherricheen on twitter (page 36)
- @samjstirling on twitter (page 37)
- @WeDoNotLearn73 on twitter (page 38)
- @Mativenko80 on twitter (page 39)
- @Charles_HRH on twitter (page 40)
- @Downwithcroiss1 (page 41)
- @GinJarNuts on twitter (page 42)
- @KatKinLee on twitter (page 43)
- @latimeralder on twitter (page 44)
- @Rachael_Swindon on twitter (page 45)
- @IanDunt on twitter (page 47)
- @LimitedThorns on twitter (page 48)
- @richardm680923 on twitter (page 49)

- @romy_gill on twitter (page 54)
- James Acaster (page 55)
- @julianpopov on twitter (page 56)
- Stephen Hawking (page 57)
- @RossalynWarren on twitter (page 58)
- @Nick_Pettigrew on twitter (page 59)
- @HUNTARmusic on twitter (page 60)
- @ReinH on twitter (page 61)
- @NerdAndProudxP on twitter (page 62)
- Conan O'Brien (page 65)
- @Rangapv on twitter (page 66)
- @thousam94 on twitter (page 67)
- Gary Lineker (page 70)
- @DFielding101 (page 71)
- @JoshuaYJackson on twitter (page 72)
- @erinmallorylong on twitter (page 77)
- @ellie_henman on twitter (page 78)
- @Pringster78 on twitter (page 79)
- @latimeralder on twitter (page 81)
- @paolaenergya on twitter (page 82)
- @SamGouldson on twitter (page 83)
- @MatthewStanger on twitter (page 85)
- @DrDavidGK on twitter (page 86)
- @charlvtte on twitter (page 88)
- @oberon_le on twitter (page 89)
- @Otto_English on twitter (page 90)
- @sarky_sheena on twitter (page 91)
- @fredrik_reuter on twitter (page 93)
- @JarvisDupont on twitter (page 95)
- Kae Kurd (page 100)
- @_Rav22 on twitter (page 105)
- @EddieHughes4WN on twitter (page 106)
- @Pjotre7 on twitter (page 107)
- @MaxineMaxbax2 on twitter (page 108)
- @BlondieJanner on twitter (page 109)

about *idiocratea*

idiocratea is an imprint of Polygon Publishing LTD. with our constantly expanding selection of trendy mugs, meme related products, gag gifts, personalised items and our very own range of original books, we at *idiocratea* pride ourselves on selling extraordinary gifts for extraordinary people.

check us out on instagram (@idiocratea_ and @polygon.publishing) and don't forget to browse our stores at **www.idiocratea.com** and **www.polygonpublishing.com**.

about the contributors

nathan bragg

nathan bragg is a uk-based digital marketing specialist, entrepreneur and lover of memes.

theresa vogrin

theresa vogrin is an austrian writer, living in the uk. she published her debut poetry book *Bitter-Sweet* in july 2018.

check out theresa's work on instagram (@theresa_vogrin) and facebook.

www.ingramcontent.com/pod-product-compliance
Lightning Source LLC
Chambersburg PA
CBHW050954050726
47592CB00007B/2571

* 9 7 8 1 9 1 6 3 7 4 0 0 3 *